GOD LOVES "BUTS"

Musings from a Misfit

by

CARMEN WILSON

WARRIOR
PUBLISHING
™

God Loves Buts: Musings of a Misfit

©2025 Karmen Thomassy

Paperback ISBN: 978-1-969202-03-2; Ebook ISBN: 978-1-969202-05-6

Hardback ISBN: 978-1-969202-04-9

Editor: Donna Bess

Publisher: Light Warrior Publishing

Editorial liberties: Names of God and references to Him are capitalized, and satan and the enemy are lowercased.

Scripture: Unless otherwise indicated, all Scripture references are from ESV: the English Standard Version, Crossway, 2001; New International Version (NIV)Holy Bible, New International Version®, NIV® Copyright ©1973, 1978, 1984, 2011 by Biblica, Inc.® Used by permission. All rights reserved worldwide.

Disclaimer: The conversations in this book all come from the author's recollections. They are not written to represent word-for-word transcripts. Rather, the author has re-told them in a way that evokes the feeling and meaning of what was said. In all instances, the essence of the dialogue is a close and accurate account of what took place. The author has changed the names of several individuals and places and may have changed some identifying characteristics and details for the protection of many in this book.

Dedication

My husband,

You are the only person I truly want to impress. I cannot fathom life without you. You are my person.

My children,

All the clichés about motherhood are true. My heart was like an old black-and-white TV with an aluminum foil-covered antenna until you came along. Instantly, my heart and vision became like a high-definition technicolor lens through which to see the world.

My Lord,

You pulled me from the miry pit and set me free.

Table of Contents

Foreword

It's not every day you meet someone who is equal parts wit and wisdom, grit and grace. I met Carmen Wilson two years ago, and from the very beginning, I knew she was someone uniquely marked by God. Carmen has this rare gift: she tells the truth—unfiltered, unpolished, and utterly refreshing. Her voice is raw yet redemptive, messy yet meaningful. She owns her story without shame and invites others to do the same.

In *GOD LOVES "BUTS": Musings from a Misfit*, Carmen brings her whole self to the page. With honesty that will make you laugh out loud and then pause to reflect, she reminds us that God is not intimidated by our contradictions. He's not put off by our "buts"— those broken places, doubts, or detours. In fact, He often does His best work right there.

As I read through this book, I found myself nodding in agreement, laughing at the absurdities of life, and, more importantly, feeling seen. Carmen's writing dismantles the lie that you have to have it all together to be used by God. She teaches us that misfits make some of the best messengers. Her words will inspire you to embrace your imperfections, rediscover God's grace in unexpected ways, and lean into the beautiful tension of being both a work in progress and deeply loved.

Whether you feel like an outsider, a wanderer, or simply someone trying to make sense of life and faith, this book will speak to you. Carmen's journey is not just hers—it's all of ours. Because at the end of the day, we all have a "but"… and thank God, He loves them.

So lean in, laugh loud, and let this book remind you of the liberating truth: you don't have to be perfect to be profoundly loved.

With love and gratitude,

Dr. Trudy Simmons
Ironman Champion, Counselor, Speaker, Host of *The Christian View*

Psalm 13

[1]How long, O Lord? Will you forget me forever?
How long will you hide your face from me?
[2] How long must I take counsel in my soul and
have sorrow in my heart all the day?
How long shall my enemy be exalted over me?

[3] Consider and answer me, O Lord my God;
light up my eyes, lest I sleep the sleep of death,
[4] lest my enemy say, "I have prevailed over him,"
lest my foes rejoice because I am shaken.

[5] **<u>But</u>** I have trusted in your steadfast love;
my heart shall rejoice in your salvation.
[6] I will sing to the Lord,
because he has dealt bountifully with me.

Credit: Dan Botan

Musing One
MY MISFIT MUSINGS

Have you ever looked around at your life and thought, "Whose story am I living?" Like you accidentally stepped into someone else's screenplay where you're expected to smile, behave, and play your part, even when your soul is itching to cry or take flight. Maybe you've been labeled: too much, too quiet, too complicated, too sensitive. Or maybe, like me, you've been caught in the tension of being mostly nice with just enough rebellion to feel like a misfit. If you've ever questioned where you belong or who you're becoming, you're not alone. This is my story—and maybe, in some way, it's yours too.

This book is a collection of my musings—a lifeline for misfits, deep feelers, and the quietly rebellious souls who've always suspected the mold was overrated anyway. If you've ever wished for permission to ditch the labels, ignore the shoulds, and just be unapologetically you, consider this your permission slip—and maybe your survival guide.

I am the odd and unconventional result of the union between an alcoholic, atheistic, temperamental Tennessee hillbilly and an uptight, overly-anxious, teetotaling, evangelical Midwesterner. Believe me, it is not as fun as it sounds.

I used to run a dog grooming salon with my friend. The most popular breed we groomed was a Labradoodle, a hybrid mix between a Labrador and a Poodle. The desired result is the sweet and friendly temperament of the Labrador combined with the intelligence and minimal shedding of the Poodle. I identify more with a "Chug"— a chihuahua/pug mix. I have the high-strung anxiety and general dislike of people like a chihuahua mixed with the lazy energy of a pug. Did I get the pious self-discipline of my mother mixed with my father's sense of adventure and love of learning? That's a hard no. The best I can offer is that I love Jesus deeply, but I appreciate a well-placed curse word.

Kevin Leman has written several books on how birth order impacts your personality. However, my place in the family order does not meet his protocol, further confirming my unusual hybrid status. I am the baby of six, kind of, in the family. As the only girl, I was raised as an only child. From early on, my family has been "blended." Even in my fifties, I am still trying to figure myself out.

Imagine the aftermath of an automobile accident with glass shards and twisted metal littering the center of an intersection, all blended together in chaos. This collage of carnage was the result of my mother getting remarried to a man with four sons when I was seven years old. My own brother left for college when I was in fifth grade, and my stepbrothers only visited sporadically. This unusual configuration made me the sole focus of my overbearing parents.

Every other weekend, I visited my father's house. Conveniently, his house had a completely different set of rules and expectations than my mother's house. My mother was very strict about what I was allowed to watch on TV and in movies, but she was reasonable about not having to clean my plate. My dad was extremely lenient on what entertainment I consumed but rigid about what and how much I ate. I guess the upside of straddling this parental fence is that I am hyper-aware of the nuances and expectations of the people around me.

The Bible says I am "wonderfully made." It's taken me half a century to accept that I am not a forgotten mistake. I now understand my unique perspective and realize there are so many people like me. I pray often, but I can't bring myself to go to church anymore because not only am I a cultural misfit, I am a theological one too.

I did not fit in with the other mothers when my children were in elementary school. I found most of them unrelatable. Maybe their kids were easier than mine, or they dreaded the quiet of their homes. I tried to understand their sadness but was too excited to go home to an empty house. Many of the moms attended a "sip and sob" mother's tea on the first day of kindergarten because they were so broken up about sending their precious babies to school. Me? My experience was quite different. I drove to their school with the windows down, wind in my unwashed hair, disco music blaring, and barely slowed down long enough to launch my second-born out of the minivan. Those ladies could sob all morning. This misfit was going home to the first peace and quiet I'd had in eight years.

What did I do that first day? I spent my time peeling the wallpaper off my kitchen walls in such small strips that they could have been used to paper the inside of an anthill. My level of frustration was making me lose my religion; HOWEVER, I was doing this menial task all by myself. No interruptions, no refereeing sibling kerfuffles, and it was nice to be able to hear myself think, even if I was putting a hex on the people who wallpapered my kitchen without priming it first.

As the school year progressed, I began to realize I was surrounded by a group of people who considered parenting to be an Olympic sport, and they were there to get the gold medal in all things motherhood. My low-key philosophy of life was trapped within a conclave of competitive Christian women.

However you feel set apart in your surroundings, you are not alone. Stick to who you are and what you believe to be important. Hold firm in your weirdness. If John the

Baptist can wear a camel hair tunic and eat bugs in the wilderness, I can decline an invitation to the weekly ladies' night out or hot yoga class without worrying too much about what other people think of me.

Credit: E. Vitka

Musing Two
WILL THE REAL "REAL" STAND UP?

To paraphrase a scene from *The Velveteen Rabbit*:

"Real isn't how you are made," said the Skin Horse.

"Does it hurt?" asked the Rabbit.

"Sometimes," said the Skin Horse. "It doesn't happen all at once. You become. It takes a long time. That's why it doesn't often happen to people who break easily, or have sharp edges, or who have to be carefully kept. Generally, by the time you are Real, most of your hair has been loved off, and your eyes drop out and you get loose in the joints and very shabby. But these things don't matter at all, because once you are Real, you can't be ugly."

Do we admire the perfectly packaged people or revere the Real? Our eyes are drawn to the pretty. Our hearts seek the Real.

In the age of social media, the "enviable" is ever-present before our eyes. We naturally admire and aspire to that highly curated level of productivity and presentation. Somewhere, though, a piece of our heart panics. Why can't I be a thin, professional chef who sews her kids' precious matching outfits inside my organized HGTV-worthy home?

Because I simply don't have the bandwidth. Maybe you are lucky enough to have a strong support system close by … family and friends who can lend a hand, watch the kids, or wait in the eternal school drop-off line for you. Help like that frees up your energy and time to "do it all."

However, the majority of women are scrambling to stay within the margin of mediocrity. If we focus too much on our kids, we neglect our spouses or work. The reverse is true too. There is only so much of us to go around, not to mention the pervasive encouragement to engage in "self-care," which is like trying to pour water from a cracked pitcher. How can we win a race that was never meant to be a competition sport?

Who do we look to for reassurance? Our mothers? God? Friends? The easiest gift we can impart to other women is our honesty. We look at the outside of others and compare it with the inside of ourselves. Apples and oranges. I know women who are gold-covered apples on the surface but rotten to the core. We are so busy trying to imitate the people we see as having it "all" that we miss the path in front of us. The higher we elevate and worship "influencers" or celebrities, the farther they fall in our admiration when we shouldn't have put our focus on them in the first place. Are the "Real Housewives" anything close to "real"? Many of them are in unhappy relationships, living above their financial means, while some have been convicted of illegal activity. Being exposed isn't the same as being honest. What do we do when the life we are living seems to fall short compared to "everyone else?" The solution is authenticity, but that feels so vulnerable.

We all need honesty, acceptance, camaraderie, and community. What would happen if we just stopped pretending that everything is perfect? I'll be the canary in the coal mine of moms and wives and risk being honest. Who is with me?

Join me as I unleash my Real, and maybe you can relate.

I've been married for over thirty years. I can't remember how many times we went to marriage counseling, but the first time was after only one year of marriage. So much for that oft-lauded "honeymoon phase." Were we the only newlyweds who struggled to figure it out so soon after getting married?

I gave birth to two of the largest babies amongst anyone I personally know. The physical damage to my body was permanent. Hello Kegels, Depends, stretch marks, and once-perfect breasts that now hang like tennis balls in a sweat sock.

My relationship with my father was so fractured that the day he died, I didn't even cry. In fact, I never cried.

Breastfeeding. What a nightmare. Do what works for you and don't worry about it.

My house has never been clean. I can 100% go to bed with dirty dishes in the sink. Even as an adult, I have to consciously force myself to close cabinets and put things in their actual place. After my son was born, I literally had breast milk stains on my bedroom carpet. I don't see that discussed on TikTok. When my kids were little, our house looked like a live-action version of *Toy Story*.

My kids entered kindergarten at six years old not knowing how to read, and frankly, they weren't interested. I am the child of a reading teacher who taught me to read at four. I did not have the energy to force them to sit with flash cards like my friends did. Guess what? Both kids did learn to read and graduated from college.

Despite spending their entire K-12 educations in Christian private schools and church, these two children curse like Marines at Boot Camp.

My body is a constant battle. I grow bone spurs like mushrooms on a rainy summer day in Georgia. I have enough scars from multiple surgeries to go as a patchwork quilt for Halloween. My knees sound like a car driving over broken glass. If I walk past the bakery section in Publix, I gain weight. I've slept a total of six hours since 1978. Bifocals. A weak bladder. I need subtitles on the TV because it all sounds like the *Peanuts* teacher. Fibromyalgia, a receding hairline, plantar fasciitis, arthritis, and anxiety are also on the Diagnosis Multipass I hold.

My list of "Real" could go on for pages. My point is that it doesn't do us any good to strive for perfection. Perfect is the enemy of good. Is it too cliché to lean into the oft-prescribed "attitude of gratitude?" The things we should praise and brag about are the amazing friends we have, family, pets, projects, hurdles cleared, and struggles overcome. If we only admire the fake façade, we start to feel ugly. And as The Velveteen Rabbit says, "Once you are real, you can't be ugly."

Credit: Sixteen Miles Out (Unsplash)

Musing Three
LETTER TO MY 9-YEAR-OLD SELF

Girlfriend, there's some stuff I have to tell you.

1. Step AWAY from the baby oil at the pool. You are Scottish and German. You will NEVER have the deep, dark tan that you covet on other girls. Go find some SPF 8 (probably the highest they had in 1979) and put it on religiously. Also, do NOT spray Sun-In on your hair. Orange is not a good look.

2. Since we're talking about hair … that is quite the rat's nest you have. The next time your mother comes near you with scissors, run, lock your door, and don't come out. Unfortunately, your hair is about to get even worse once puberty hits. Your middle school years will be recorded with the ugliest school photos … ever. Your hair is frizzy, and a good product hasn't been invented. Stop trying to Farrah-Fawcett-flip it. There are only a few girls who can pull this look off, and you are not

one of them. The cowlick you have will eventually go away, and guess what? When you are in your thirties, you will have lovely hair. You will pay a fortune for it, and it will be worth every penny. Then, there is your body. After school, quit eating like it's your last meal. You are starting bad habits that I still have to contend with. You are active now roller skating, skateboarding, and swimming, but those knees can't hang on forever because you have bad DNA and paper-thin cartilage that will ultimately require cortisone shots. I'll spare you the details of the double hip replacement you will have before you turn fifty.

3. The clothes you have on are appalling, but it's all your parents can afford. They are trying to support six kids, and you are the last one. They don't understand that your Buster Brown shoes or Goodwill pants make you a target for the Mean Girls. The good news is that when you are older, you will be satisfied with less. The Target clearance rack will be your "Happy Place," and you will not need name-brand clothes. Your friends will love you despite your clothes, and you will feel sorry for people who literally go into debt to have a name-brand purse to flaunt.

4. Boys. Sigh.
   You are going to enter some awful relationships. I am tempted to tell you to run, but I won't. The

guys that threatened and yelled at you or simply didn't treat you kindly will teach you one of the most important lessons in life: to recognize a good man and marry him. Also, you aren't the nicest person either. You will break some hearts and be mean-spirited. I would love to tell you to treat those decent boys with respect and consideration, but you are stubborn and need to be humbled by your actions so that you will be a better person in the end. When you meet your future husband, you will take a deep breath and exhale with relief. He will be your soft place to fall.

5.   Your parents. Double sigh.
      In general, they are doing the best they can. One day, you will be a parent and make equally bad decisions, act out of anger, and be selfish. You will learn to forgive most of their mistakes. The ones you struggle to forgive will play a role in making you a better mother. You and your brother are collateral damage in their custody agreement. The arrangement is that your father will pull up, toot the horn, and you better scatter like a cockroach, grab your suitcase, and get your rear in gear out to his idling car.
      No.
      Unacceptable.
      Get off the couch and tell your mother, who is hiding in her room so she doesn't have to see him,

that you will not sit in the bay window like a pet store animal and wait. When he gets there, tell him that a gentleman comes to the door for a lady, regardless of her age. You will most likely get chewed out by both of them, but it'll be worth it. Too bad it won't happen. You won't understand the complete ridiculousness of what's going on until you are older and have a master's degree in counseling.

6. Pets. I know you really want a horse. You even subscribe to the *Quarter Horse Association* magazine. You will never be given a lesson, so quit asking them. They don't have the money, time, or desire to drive you for a lesson. It's okay. In the future, your little girl will want a horse, and you will see the wisdom in buying one. It will, hands down, be the best parenting decision you make. Coincidentally, he will be a Quarter Horse. See, some dreams actually come true. I know you also want a dog. One day, you will fall head over heels in love with a wrinkly-faced, bad-breathed, anal-gland-releasing pug, and he will be the secret love of your life.

7. As you go through puberty, you will experience menstrual cramps that will be debilitating. I have no advice except to say that the pain of those cramps will seem like a trip to the nail salon once you go into labor for the first time. It's all about perspective. The birth of your second child, a

twelve-pound baby/toddler delivered via C-section with the epidural shut off, will reset your pain tolerance to "I wish a bus would run me over 1,000 times,"

8. It's 1979, and you are having a hard time. You are prone to rage-filled outbursts; you are negative and complain a lot. You have trouble sleeping (sorry to tell you, that will never improve. Insomnia sucks.) and have begun to pull your eyelashes out. Let me give you the cold, hard truth: this is not entirely the result of your living arrangements, your parents' divorce, or any other external circumstance. You are an anxiety-filled, negative person. It's your personality. The good news is that as you get older, you will be able to make that negativity work for you and not against you. People will find your musings refreshing or scary, but entertaining nonetheless. The ultimate kicker is that you will give birth to a child of equal negativity, irritability, and anxiousness. Sorry. It's the circle of life. What no one in your family wants to admit is that you come from a long line of hand-wringing, high-strung nervous Nellies. It's not your fault, it's just who you are. Get some therapy and learn not to steal other people's joy with your anxiety and negativity. It CAN be done. Good luck with that kid you will have. I have no advice for you; I'm still figuring him out.

9. You are going to learn some hard lessons about people and ultimately about yourself. While it is natural to judge people based on external factors, fight that urge. Most of the time, you will be wrong, despite all the hours you will sit in psychology classes learning how to read people. In fact, you suck at it. You will meet attractive, well-educated, and articulate people who have zero integrity and character. You will also meet people that you automatically discount based on their differences from you. I'm glad to report that you will learn the error of your ways, you will invite some colorful people of various backgrounds into your life, and you will be deeply enriched by them. Go on the journey with people. Be a little more reserved, and at the same time, open your heart and mind to see people. Have thick skin but a soft heart. God made each person on this earth, and every one of them has a story and uniqueness about them. You are not qualified to judge. You never will be, so relax and have fun. By the way, you don't want people judging you based on your appearance. Look at yourself, unshowered, disheveled and wearing leggings as pants with Kohl's clearance rack baggy shirts covering your bum.

10. Ultimately, the message I want you to know is that in the end, it's going to be okay. Despite the trials

and tribulations, you are going to survive the devastating broken hearts, physical ailments, loneliness, and anxiety that are coming your way. You will have a family and friends, pets, and ultimately peace. It's your job to stay on the path and find it before it's too late.

Credit: Erik McLean (Unsplash)

Musing Four
SHOULD

I once heard a Social Work professor say that we "shouldn't **SHOULD** on each other."

Ouch.

I confess that I am so guilty of *shoulding* on people. I probably did it yesterday and will possibly do it today ... although I should not. I am a World Class *should*-er.

I had an epiphany this weekend. I'll call it "Bricks in a Backpack." What happens is so simple and common. Someone will read a book, a LIFE-CHANGING book ... the book they've been waiting for their whole lives. Now that they've read this book, they know things, have insight, and are REALLY excited to tell you about this book.

The conversation tends to go like this: "I just read THE BEST BOOK. EVER. You HAVE to read it!!!"

And there goes another brick in my backpack that is already heavy. Something else I "HAVE" to do.

Like the word *should*, its impact doesn't match the intent. The intent is to share an amazing opportunity, experience, recipe, book, Bible verse, exercise, or diet that has brought someone out of the pit. It has changed them, and they are sure it will help you feel better, enlighten you, etc. The problem is, our loads are already heavy. I think most of us are doing the best we can with what we have. I am so guilty of doing this to people. For example, I have been seeing a naturopath for about a year. She is amazing. AMAZING. You HAVE to call her! What I should say is, "I have been seeing someone, and I feel so much better." That's it. No more.

I've been feeling heavy for the last year. Not physically heavy—which I am, and believe me, I KNOW if I go gluten-free, candida-free, carb-free, drink a glass of wine, lift weights, eat vegetarian or vegan, I'll no doubt be a new person. Except, I just can't. Not today. Maybe tomorrow. But today, I'm just a girl trying to stay afloat. So, when people tell me:

I should go on the Ladies' Bible Retreat

I should write in a journal

I should use this supplement for my horse

I should join this gym

I should eat that … or don't eat this

I should pray more

I should read this version of that book

I should attend this meeting

I should go on a marriage retreat

I should get a rescue horse/dog, but not that dog, or this dog.

I feel overwhelmed by the input of mostly well-meaning people trying to help.

As you read all the *shoulds*, aren't you annoyed? This list doesn't help, and it only adds more bricks to the backpack of what I am already NOT doing, but should. Ugh, I am guilty of lobbing the Bricks of Should at other people.

I've been *should* on a lot in the last few weeks. My backpack is heavy. The only way I can make it lighter is to make a commitment to stop saying to other people, "You have to try this, read this, see this person, eat this," and instead, to just say, "Wow, I just read the most interesting article in the paper." Now, you don't have to carry that heavy brick around, and you won't hand it to someone else.

I think social media has added ten pounds to each brick of *should* we carry around. It's so easy to go online and tell people who and what they *should*—vote for, oppose, hate, like, support, where to eat, or boycott. I wish I knew the right balance. Sometimes I will read something or try something and think, *"Why didn't someone tell me about this earlier?"* But I am starting to think that we find our own way, in our own time, when we are ready.

I hope I can break this bad habit and extend grace and mercy to those who *should* on me as well.

Credit: Virginia Thomassy

Musing Five
THE LONG GAME

I like efficiency. Give me a video with "life hacks," and I'll watch it every time to see how I can get a task done with the least amount of time and energy. "Work smarter, not harder" is my motto, or maybe I'm just lazy. My GPS app gets used daily, even for routes I take all the time; maybe today there is an even better (i.e. quicker) way, whether it's a shortcut or avoiding some unexpected congestion. If you want to see me lose my religion, put a cyclist or construction crew on my curvy country road.

When I go to dinner, I have already read the menu and know what I'm going to order, and while you're at it, can you bring me the check with the entrée? Recently, I went to dinner with a group of friends, and there was a pay station at the table where you could not only pay your bill at your earliest convenience, but you could even divide up the check per item. Efficiency heaven!

The point I am belaboring is—I don't like to wait when I don't have to.

Enter the God who created heaven and earth (was it really in six days? because A+ for efficiency). I have begrudgingly accepted that God likes to play the long game. And I mean L-O-N-G.

In the New Testament, there is the story of Zaccheus, the short statured tax collector who wanted a better look at Jesus as He was passing through Jerusalem. According to Scripture, he climbed a sycamore tree, and as Jesus passed by, He called out to Zaccheus to come down and spend time with him. I read a quote that says, "Long before Zaccheus couldn't see Jesus, the tree was already planted to meet his need." Sycamore trees get to full maturity between fifty and two hundred years and can live up to four hundred years. Did God plant a sycamore tree four hundred years before Zaccheus needed it? Talk about playing the long game.

My daughter owns a corgi, a breed of dog with small legs and big opinions. One day, while she was walking him around the park, he became tired and stubborn, not wanting to take the next step. What he could not see that she could was that the car was right around the bend. Just a few more minutes and the rest he craved was his for the taking. How do you reason with a dog that their journey is so close to coming to an end? I guess you can't.

What about us? If I were giving God a Yelp review, I would register my complaint about "time of service." The waiting room can feel eternal when The Doctor lives in eternity. Our earthly sense of time is so limited that it feels painful against the backdrop of infinity. Oftentimes, when I have been made to wait, sometimes for years, hindsight helps me to understand God's timing. The delay wasn't a denial of my prayers; it was God saying that He had something better in store. Better? Why wait for 100% when I would happily settle for 75%? I suppose because God won't give us "less than." Pastor and author Craig Cooney writes, "The enemy will offer you an 'almost' to distract and divert from God's best."

Like Zaccheus and the corgi, I have short legs. Maybe those of us with short legs are extra tired because we have to take two steps for a normal person's one stride. When I was in my early twenties, before my knees started to look like Swiss cheese and sound like Rice Krispies, I took up jogging with a friend. She was in shape and accustomed to running miles at a time. On our first outing, I insisted that I could not run more than a mile or so. She gently suggested that we jog "to that tree," then "that tree" became the bend on the pond, and so on. We took walk breaks, but as soon as I caught my breath, she encouraged me to keep running, often saying that the parking lot was close. She was lying like a rug.

Because I did not know where the car was, I trusted her and kept running, thinking it would be over soon. In the end, I jogged about five miles. If you had asked me if I was physically capable of running that far, I would have emphatically denied it. I just didn't know what I was capable of, and in this situation, ignorance was bliss. I was so proud of myself that I forgot to be mad at my friend for tricking me into running so far.

Back to the corgi: he was focused on his fatigue and had to submit to his owner, whereas I had to have faith in my friend. The corgi and I both had to blindly rely on who was guiding us back home.

How often do we give up because the long game seems too long? How far could we go if we trusted God and just kept moving forward? I wish I had answers. Weariness and hopelessness can be soul killers, and I often wear both like a matching set of weighted shoes. If I knew how close the reward was, I'd keep on keeping on. However, God doesn't want me looking forward; He wants me looking up at Him. But, if I'm looking at Him, I fear that I may trip. On the flip-side, if I saw how far away the finish line was, I'd most likely give up and stay still. Maybe even turn back around. This is the human experience—trying to run a spiritual race on a physical plane with no map or Siri to tell me how far away my destination is.

Seems inefficient, right? God isn't concerned with life hacks or Easy Street when He's planting trees hundreds of years in advance. Trusting God to take us home via the long way is really hard.

Credit: Noor Younis

Musing Six
BE CAREFUL WHAT YOU WISH FOR

Since 1997, I've dreamed of FREE TIME!

I made lists, real and imagined, about how organized, interesting, well-read, and thin I would be if I just had TIME. My house would be clean—windows to baseboards, recipes organized, dogs walked, cars washed, counters crumb-free, nails polished, gifts bought, newspapers/magazines/books devoured, laundry washed, folded, and put away.

Instead, I feel like a dead weight. Things get done, not with fervor but only so I can cross something—anything—off my to-do list, so that when I settle into my La-Z-Boy chair, I can alleviate a half ounce of guilt when the *Law and Order* marathon begins.

I throw the ball for the dog while sitting on my porch—that's exercise, right? I text friends and talk on the phone. I even "lunch." I'm not literally in my basement with the blinds drawn for days. However, in my head and heart, I am figuratively in the basement, under the covers, numbing my mind with insignificant things.

Am I insignificant?

My family has been my life for decades. I have ZERO regrets about spending every possible minute on them. They are flourishing. The kids have grown into fine, independent people, and my husband has the freedom to work wherever and whenever he needs without worrying about things at home.

Now … it's MY TIME.

Instead of tackling the undone chores, tasks, and errands of the last two decades, I am hunkered down and fighting back tears at every turn. My daughter got a job in Europe for the summer, and my heart felt like it was going to shrivel up. While she was gone, I started having trouble flossing between my molars. I went to the dentist and discovered that my teeth have literally shifted due to clenching them during her absence trying to keep the tears from flowing freely. How could I go from disco dancing on the first day of kindergarten to being a weepy mess during their teen years only a decade later?

Maybe I thought an organized recipe folder, thinner thighs, and a mildew-free bathroom would be an equal substitution for my purpose as a mother. The changes—the assault of hours of uninterrupted time—have blown the lid off my belief of how I would/could/should be if I just had enough "free time."

Apparently, time is proving to reveal a tired, sad, unfocused, out-of-shape, and disorganized person. Pretty much the person I was before this twenty-year "interruption."

Yet, I have to believe with all my heart that God has bigger plans for me than to while away my time on my couch as life moves around me. For the moment, I will just BE. I will be sad, lazy, weepy, unmotivated, and chunky. I know I must pass through this place on my way to better things. So, until then, I will wait on the Lord.

Credit: Annie Gavin (Unsplash)

Musing Seven
HOPES, DREAMS, AND FANTASIES

"Hope itself is like a star—not to be seen in the sunshine of prosperity, and only to be discovered in the night of adversity" —Charles Spurgeon

Hope is that faint light that shines far off in the distance. Just keep inching toward the ray of light to find your way out of the darkness. The light from a single match can pierce the pitch black enough to show the shadows of obstacles to avoid and the promise of brighter things ahead. It may be a tedious task, and your movements will be cautious to ensure your safety, but at least you know which direction to travel.

Dreams can bathe you in enough light for a quicker journey and a clearer goal. The brightness from a flashlight will illuminate the path ahead, showing what impediments to dodge. You will also see clearly enough to make a detailed plan for fulfillment and the fastest route to satisfaction.

Fantasies are so bright that you can't see how to travel to the endpoint. While hopes and dreams provide a basic blueprint, fantasies are near impossibilities—winning the lottery, miracle healings, being "discovered" for a dream job while you are making your Starbucks run. You must travel beyond the path of reason to victory.

I realized years ago, as my kids needed me less and I turned my focus back on myself, that I didn't have any dreams, goals, desires, and frankly, very little hope for personal growth and new adventures. Like many children from a broken or dysfunctional family system, my primary coping mechanism was putting to death my dreams, big and small. I saw having dreams as a fool's errand, a luxury for the well-loved and supported. Dreaming only led to deep disappointment. When you are nine, adulthood feels like a lifetime away. It's hard to grasp that one day, you will have enough independence and vision to bring your dreams into existence. As a child, you are at the mercy of every adult in your life—grown-ups who have lost sight of their own aspirations. Most of whom were just struggling to get through their daily responsibilities. The drudgery of adulthood gave them amnesia about the beauty of a youthful mind that sees the world as full of possibilities. As a result, they either intentionally or accidentally squashed their children's dreams.

I was so desperate for a lifeline—that light from a single flame to guide me to the exit door where I could be free. Squinting for years upon years dims your eyesight, even blinding some people to the point that they quit looking for a tiny beacon to lead them through the door of hopes and dreams.

Surely, personality type can influence your perseverance in pursuing better outcomes for your life. There are those of us realists that accept the situation quickly. Acceptance of "what is" and moving on is the only way to realistically deal with the despair of dashed dreams. In the moment, we learn important coping skills: head down, don't dream, get through the day. On the other end of the spectrum are the *creators*. They tend to fail more frequently but bounce back like prize-fighters willing to take another hit on their way to victory. The *creators* operate outside of the box that the *realists* resigned themselves to exist in for emotional safety.

I've heard that a bonsai tree can actually grow into a full-sized tree. To keep them small and manageable, all one has to do is keep them in a small container, trim their roots, and remove the leaves. The limitation of its growth isn't natural, but early conditioning and constant pruning keep it from reaching its full potential.

Like the bonsai, that early cutting and containing forced an adaptation that caused some of us to struggle with the autonomy of adulthood. When the confines of our familial boxes have been long-gone and we have liberty and financial stability, we still hold on to the imaginary anchors of security and predictability.

The refuge we seek actually harms our spirit. While losing or denying our ability to dream serves its purpose in the short run, as adults we are left floundering and flopping around in our freedom. The fear of disappointment is so intense and triggering that we don't even try. If we do branch out and dip a toe into the wishing well, we cut and run at the first sign of difficulty. On red alert, we scan the horizon miles away for impending dangers and deterrents, anticipating failure with intense anxiety. We quit, choosing to surrender on "our own terms" as opposed to feeling the sting of a dream deferred or disappeared.

I have given a lot of thought as to why I don't ponder future possibilities. I realized that I do allow myself to fantasize. With fantasies there is no real danger of disappointment. No one expects a miracle to actually happen. Instead of putting effort into formulating a plan for "better" that could come to fruition, I disappear mentally into a world where I can safely create scenarios that are so unlikely I might as well write a speech for my Oscar nomination or make space for my Nobel prize.

I am trying to move forward into a healthy place where I can allow myself to visualize true growth and change. Why is it so hard??? I've been doing an exercise in my head where I write down:

The Hope: which is vague at best.
The Dream: which has a finish line and the chance to happen.
The Fantasy: which has almost zero statistical odds of occurring.

The dreams are the scariest for me.

WHAT IF:

It doesn't happen?
I try my absolute hardest and I fail?
"It" just isn't in the cards for me?
I look stupid or delusional?

How do I wrap this up with a pretty bow? How can I master my deep fear of disappointment? Can you relate? I want to hold on to my false sense of safety by refusing to hope and dream. I lie to myself that by holding back from God, I am insulating myself from being let down. Intellectually and theologically, I know this does not work.

In an act of vulnerability, I have been writing my desires in my prayer journal—unclenching fists that hold hidden dreams, letting my pencil record on paper what God reveals to me and relearning the child-like belief that anything is possible.

Credit: Marissa Lewis (Unsplash)

Musing Eight
WHITE

A while back, I asked a wise friend, "Do you think God is complicated or simple?"

She answered, "Both. Look at a simple cell. It is the basis for all things … so simple, and yet, when you look at the workings and systems inside one single cell, it's complicated. I think God is like that."

Black AND White.

How many of us long to live in the black and white, where everything seems simple and clear? But is it? Is the space between black and white actually gray?

Not really.

I told my mentor/therapist/counselor/guru (you will notice a pattern that NOTHING is as simple as one label) that I felt like God had plopped me in a giant, gray puddle to find my way out. How I long for the black and white. For clarity. No wiggle room. The Law.

She said, "Do you know what's in between the black and white? Not gray, but the rainbow." Hmmmm. So, I am starting to research the simplicity and complexity of color. Much like God, color is simple and complex.

Is white a color? Well, that depends. Can anything have a clear answer? There is color as light, color as pigment, and color as reflection. Who knew? In terms of light, black is NOT a color, it is the absence of light. However, white as light is the combination of ALL colors. The reverse tends to be true when discussing pigment. Black is the combination of the primary colors (red, blue, yellow). So it is a color.

Confused yet? Even in the perception of color we must ponder, ask, research and seek. I take so many things as I "see" them, not necessarily as they are. I was "seeing" my life as a gray morass of "in between" when God was actually injecting all the colors around me, but I had to find them. And believe me, it's been hard.

White: Purity, Cleanliness, Holiness.

White is the color desired by brides and dreaded by mothers. How long can white stay white? The smallest, ill-placed stain can ruin the longest white dress. Is the same true for our souls? Simply put, yes. Complexly, no.

God says that one sin separates us from Him.

One. Sin. (Psalm 53:3; Romans 3:23.)

Uh-Oh.

In a nutshell, we are all brides wearing a dress with a wine stain on the front. How do we keep the white … white? Vigilance, Alertness, Dedication, Steadfastness. But those actions are so tiring! Have you ever tried to keep your toddler's white garment stain-free before the photo op? As a bride, you must keep a sharp eye out for any sloshing drinks, limo grease, or dust. Here's the worst part about white. Even if you are ultra-careful and manage to never drop a crumb on that white shirt, the dreaded pit stains eventually appear.

We sweat. We sin. We stain.

Where is the hope? For clothing, our hope is found in the power of Clorox, a substance that also, if mishandled, can ruin something else in the process of bleaching a stain! Once again, a misplaced drop of bleach on your black rug, navy jacket, or red pants spells ruin.

What about our souls? Ironically, the way to keep our souls white, pure, and clean is to cover ourselves in the crimson blood of Christ.

God is full of mysteries and ironies. The only way to a pure heart is by the shed blood of another human. Human blood is dirty, full of diseases like HIV, hepatitis, and malaria. We see biohazard boxes in every single doctor's office. One drop of human blood can contaminate or even kill another human. And yet, our simple and complex God took on a human form and was filled with God's pure blood to cleanse us.

Confused??? The point is, we MUST constantly be seeking Him. Asking Him. He reveals the truth to us; things are not always as they seem. In conclusion, we know that white is all the colors combined within light. "I am the way, the truth, and the light" (John 14:6), and even one stain can ruin white. There is hope though because God will use the red blood of His Son to get the stains out of our hearts.

Credit: Mitya Ivanov

Musing Nine
STAINED-GLASS HOUSES

"Do not judge (*krinos*) or you too will be judged" (Matthew 7:1).

"Do not judge (*krinos*) by appearance, but judge with right judgment" (John 7:24).

The Greek word for judge is *krinos*. In the book of Matthew, we are told not to judge other people because the same standards will be used on us. Three books later in the gospel of John, we read not to judge based on looks, but we should judge using the correct criteria. To sum it up, don't judge because you'll be judged, but also when you do judge, make sure you are using good judgment. You can see how it is easy to misunderstand and misinterpret what God is asking of us.

When I try to make "sense" out of God, I feel like a five-year-old trying to figure out quantum physics. The character, complexity, compassion and composition of God is beyond my comprehension. And yet … we are called to stay in constant communication with Him. An invitation to sit at the holy feet of the Father should wow and excite me into action. However, maintaining an open dialogue has proven to be a challenge for me.

Why?

First of all, I would have to LISTEN.

Ew.

It's easier for me to go to God with my prepared prayer list in hand to repent and recite than it is for me to receive His message. Silence is uncomfortable. In an effort to increase my spiritual status and standing, it is more tempting to emulate another person I deem to be more righteous. Better to follow the example of Baptist Betty or Catholic Cathy than to sit in monk-like solitude waiting for God to speak to me. The problem with following people instead of God is obvious. The preachers, politicians, and pro-athletes we put on a pedestal become our modern equivalent of the Old Testament golden calves that vexed Moses. When we follow denominational doctrine or godly "gurus," we are bypassing the intimacy God expects and desires from us. One of the hardest lessons I have learned is that God is calling each one of us into a private conversation with Him.

Our concept of God is more comprehendible when we put Him in a container of our own making. The Bible is God's Word for His people, but we have flipped the script and used it as The People's Guide to God. We limit God's actions, motives, and rules (oh, how we LOVE the rules!) within the pages edited by man. For added fun, we weaponize certain verses to pass judgment, excommunicate, and nitpick those who experience God in a different way. Just as God intended. *This is when I wish there was a sarcasm font.*

While God made us in His image, we were given the free will to be and act as we wish. Humans are a complicated bunch—fickle, immature, irresponsible, and/or controlling. We can have the tendency to be judgy, joyless hall monitors. The cure for these character flaws is communion with God.

Instead, we don the lens of legality and decide for ourselves who is right, wrong, left, loose, pious, or pure. The Pharisees spent all their energy displaying their righteous ranking. They maintained their pious pecking order by only caring about appearances (see John 7:24) and forgot about the heart.

Over and over, the Trinity reminds us that our focus should be to love God and love His people, in that order.

It takes a lot of effort, humility, self-reflection, and emotional heavy lifting to stay committed to those two commandments. Wouldn't it be simpler to sit back and decide who and what is "right" instead of waiting on the nuanced word of the Lord? If I am concentrating on what God is saying to me, I won't have the time and energy to fight over which denomination has the "right" rites. Christianity is plagued by endless inter-denominational fighting over communion, skirt length, women's roles, hymns, purity, sexuality, confession, tithing, etc. Entire churches have split over lesser issues. There are Christian parents who do not speak to their gay children. How is this love? Any church or religion that not only encourages but demands ostracizing family members who aren't living in alignment with your particular brand of theology is exactly the opposite of:

Love God.
Love People.

We don't have to agree with someone to love them. Also, "loving" someone with the agenda of changing them is not loving them. We can wish that our alcoholic aunt or bankrupt brother makes better choices in the future, but removing love isn't going to get the message across.

The challenge with having a personal relationship with God is that it is so specific. God may call me to do or not do something different than you, and that's when tensions rise. Because we are so tribal, our attention is usually focused outward and not upward. What if God asks me to do something "weird?" What if God asks half of the ladies' Bible study group to volunteer at a shelter, but tells the other half to stay home? Who is right? What if both are correct?

I was recently corresponding with a missionary friend. He is serving in an area experiencing genocides, an influx of refugees, and a corrupt government. Truly, I admire his work there. Also, I know God is not calling me to go into a war zone. I was not wired for that environment. I am afraid of spiders and stomach bugs. I don't even camp. Driving to the airport or trying to park somewhere new sends waves of anxiety through my body. I am a weenie—and that is okay. My friend and I are both following what God has asked us to do.

God calls pioneers and settlers. My missionary friend is a pioneer, out on the front lines of a dangerous battlefield, offering peace to the people living there. Can you imagine how bored he would be with my quiet, contemplative life, the life of a settler, putting down stakes and maintaining peace?

The seeds of trouble begin sprouting when we assign different values to spiritual callings. If I see myself as doing "less than" another person, I may shrink in shame. If I assign a higher value to my calling, I will be tempted to sit in judgment of another's endeavor. Can you imagine if I attempted to move to an area of the world mired in violence and strife with my squirrelly disposition and sweaty palms? I would be of use to no one and in fact a hindrance to those better equipped to serve God there.

As humans, we want to evaluate the "kingdom impact value" of our callings, which opens the door to the judge's chamber. The fact is, we won't know the consequences of our obedience until we are in God's presence. A settler may inspire the next pioneer. A pioneer might create a safe place for a settler to find God. We may never know what God will ask us to do that will set the stage for generations to come.

Let's not forget that God has asked people to do some ODD things.

Hosea: marry a prostitute.

Jonah: preach to cannibals.

John the Baptist: a camel-hair-wearing bug-eater.

Ezekiel: cooked his food over excrement, shaved his head, and chopped up his hair with an ax.

Jeremiah: hid his loincloth under a rock in the river, wore yoke-bars when he spoke to the public.

While we are reflecting on God's A-team, He had strange taste in who He chose to represent Him.

Moses: murderer

Abraham: liar

Jacob: manipulator

Rahab: prostitute

David: (the man "after God's own heart") had someone murdered, committed adultery, his household and children were a mess

Peter: liar and denier

Paul: spent years harassing and condemning Christians

Mary Magdalene: formerly demon-possessed

Also, how many times did the twelve disciples have to be reminded that their constant companion was the actual Son of God? They were frequently bewildered by the supernatural acts He regularly performed.

So … if these are the people God has called and consecrated, maybe we should loosen the screws on the box we've built to contain God and control people. We all want to be important and included in the Kingdom of God. While Jesus referred to us as "sheep" in a parable, our true identity is that of a Child of God. I have two children. They are my whole heart, and yet my expectations, requests, and goals for them vary wildly based on their individual strengths and weaknesses. Is this not the same dynamic within the Body of Christ? However, instead of embracing our unique Kingdom callings, we criticize and attack other people. I've seen Christian entertainers called out for their choice of performing venues, tattoos, clothing, marital status ... the list is endless.

So, how do I know what God is saying to me? The answer lies in further proof that each one of us experiences God differently. God can and does speak in so many ways: visions, dreams, actual audible words, nature, a strong affinity or "pull" toward something. Along with judging someone's spiritual calling, Christians will judge the methodology of receiving that message.

One of the most popular idioms of our culture is: *People who live in glass houses shouldn't throw stones.* The stones littering the glass house I live in often entice me to toss one at someone in another denomination or lob one in the direction of people in a different political party. Those stones seem to be even more tempting if they are inside a church with stained-glass walls. Resist the urge to be distracted by what the other Christians are doing, and listen for God's voice speaking directly to you. You won't regret it.

Credit: John Price (Unsplash)

Musing Ten
YOUTH GROUP

In high school, I participated in a national Christian outreach youth group (I'll refer to it as YG). Throughout my time at YG, my heart was softened and my eyes opened to see God in a totally different way than I had been taught as a child. At the time, it was so appealing—a departure from our parents' church experience.

The majority of us Gen Xers attended church services that were dry as a bone, rote, ritualistic, and repetitive. Teenagers in the 80s and 90s gravitated to this new way of worshiping. For the first time, we heard worship songs that we could bop our heads and clap our hands to. "How Great Thou Art" is a beautiful hymn, but singing along with Michael W. Smith and Amy Grant allowed us to praise God in ways we had never experienced before. It felt fresh and alive.

We were drawn in by fun music, entertaining messages, and leaders we could identify with—many barely older than the kids they oversaw.

When I began attending meetings, I was bitter, angry, disobedient, lost, empty, and desperate for a reprieve from a very unhappy home life. This group invited me in and exposed me to the concept that God didn't have to be experienced only through boring church services and pre-written prayers mindlessly uttered in unison.

As it turns out, God is FUN, and He loves teenagers.

I made life-long friends that I still see or speak to regularly after forty years. Looking back, it is hard to imagine what my life would be like without the guidance of those leaders and the support of my fellow YG members.

I want to tread lightly as I unpack some of the negative remnants of those experiences. It's easy to criticize imperfect 1988 methods through a 2025 high-definition lens. Hindsight is 20/20. As a middle-aged, weather-worn, battle-tested Christian, I can now see some of the damaging flaws of the "Amy Grant-YG-Campus Crusade For Christ-Purity Ring" rules-based version of Christianity we were baptized into.

The religious doctrine of our parents' generation had just been repackaged in a modern tone, but the rules were still enforced using shame. I want to say that I truly believe that the majority of people involved and the institutions that were emerging at this time meant well. They had a deep desire to spread the word of God to the next generation. Their primary goal was to ensure we understood the importance of obedience to God's laws. Sadly, grace and mercy were offered as side dishes to be served once the rules were consistently kept. The underlying goal was a noble one: to keep us out of trouble. I have no doubt that many of us were able to avoid life-altering mistakes by being held accountable to the rules.

The problem humanity has always had is that blind obedience leads to a cold heart. The Pharisees competed to see who kept the law more devoutly, and Jesus couldn't stand the darkness of their hearts and the judgments on their lips. The underlying reasons why we engage in sinful and destructive behaviors weren't addressed in a youth group setting, nor could they be. YG leaders are rarely licensed therapists, and Campus Crusade volunteers are often barely adults themselves. Teenagers are a hot mess of moodiness, hormones, irresponsibility, anger, and drama—basically, large toddlers going through the most critical transformation of their lives with large helpings of sexual awareness and confusion to make matters worse.

The message we received was that God wanted to have a relationship with us but could not until we were cleansed by the blood of Christ. I heard one youth minister describe us as children covered in vomit, and God had to clean us up before He could extend His love. Obedience was sold as the only way to receive God's blessings and forgiveness. If you do good, you receive good. For example, staying a virgin until your wedding night meant a passionate sex life and a relationship blessed by God. The problem with that belief is that it is not a guarantee, nor is it a formula for receiving God's blessings. How I wish God were so easy to manipulate and predict, but He is not. Clinical psychologist John Rosemond says that "doing good things doesn't ensure that only good things will happen to you; it just reduces the chances of bad things happening to you."

Sex-shaming us was often the focus of many discussions. As future wives, we were told that if we didn't stay "pure," God would limit our potential marriage partners to men willing to lower themselves to redeem a Rahab (who interestingly was part of Jesus' lineage). How often were female Gen Xers given analogies like, "If you slip up sexually, you are like an empty tube of toothpaste with no hope of 'putting the toothpaste back in the tube,' or, "You're like a clean sheet of paper that has been crumpled?" You could unwrinkle the paper, but there would forever be the evidence of folds, no matter how hard you tried to smooth it out. While the teenage boys were also admonished to control themselves sexually, it was more important to seek out a pure wife.

These are the areas of Christianity that are difficult to unpack and communicate properly. It seems to be easier to extol the laws of God instead of the character of God. Laws are concrete; understanding character requires intimacy. God absolutely made rules, commandments, and laws for us to heed. One of the purposes of these boundaries was for our own protection. Whether it was how to handle food, do business, honor covenants, or manage money, the rules were to keep us healthy and prosperous. He didn't want to see His children mired in situations that would negatively impact their lives: addiction, adultery, abortion, diseases, jail, or lost opportunities. Like any parent, He has only wanted the best for us.

But.

But what happens when we sin and fall off the path set before us or lose our way? Why did it seem some sins were more easily "forgiven" and others required us to don our Hester Prynn scarlet A's for eternity? Can God forgive all sins, or do we need to walk around like the Opus Dei believers, self-flagellating for the world to see our contrition?

Why is the balance between grace and obedience razor-thin? We fear that giving the message that God loves us unconditionally will lead to spiritual lawlessness. When we speak of God's love and mercy, we coat it with a thick layer of fear and condemnation woven within the gospel message so we fall in line and don't sin. The critically missing pieces of the story are:

- We should enter into a relationship with God.
- Closeness with God leads to loving God.
- When we love someone, we behave in a way that honors them.

As it turns out, the Bible is filled with all kinds of characters who behaved poorly. God loved them, forgave them, used them to glorify Himself, and often spoke highly of them in the scriptures. The truth is that He loved us first. Period. We cannot do anything to change that holy dynamic. We do have the choice to accept His love or not. His laws were given to keep us safe. His grace was given to us so that we would never be separated from His love.

The Gen Xers are long grown up, most with children of their own. I have been so encouraged to see a generation rise up that seems to accept and proclaim that God loves them. God loves you, and having an intimate relationship with Him is the foundation for all other aspects of our lives.

Credit: Nick Karvounis

Musing Eleven
IF IT CUTS EARLY, IT CUTS DEEP

Even before I was a hormonal teenager, I was drawn to the dream of passionate, romantic love. It's easy to look back with my educated eyes and see what was really going on. I was a picture-perfect depiction of "daddy issues"; however, at twelve years old, I had zero self-awareness about my unhealthy need for love from a man and how to properly fulfill it. What the devil saw was *low-hanging fruit*, and I was ripe for the picking. Feeling trapped, unloved, and frustrated with my family, I escaped into movies like *The Blue Lagoon*. To be stranded on a remote, tropical island without overbearing parents and with unlimited access to a lover was the ultimate teenage fantasy.

I always had a boyfriend. When I experienced my first real break-up, the devastation was so real. As an adult, I realize that listening to a thirteen-year-old carry on about a broken heart sounds trivial, but I still remember how heavy my heart sat in my chest, like a brick of rejection. The sting of that particular break-up literally lasted for years. Even as I moved on to other relationships, that first tear in my heart was the foundation on which I piled all future rejections.

By the time I allowed God into my life as a teenager, my heart was already so damaged. The intense longing for a romantic partner to rescue me had been imprinted on my soul. While I loved God, my belief was that if I could get married, I would be whole. Enter the era of The Idol of Marriage, and we all know how God feels about idols.

When you are looking for potential partners through the lens of desperation, your vision is clouded, and God is seen only in the periphery. My focus was bisected by my love for God and my dream of getting married someday. In addition to my misguided focus on finding a husband, I was repeatedly reminded that I was already "used goods." It would surely take a man of great spiritual patience and understanding to lower himself to marry me.

Ugh. The things Christians do to each other. We don't need the devil; we have each other to judge, shame, and rebuke. I got the message that forgiveness could only be granted after deep shame had been absorbed into my spirit. This morass of my disgrace, my Christianity, and my emptiness was packed up in my suitcase and moved to college with me. The Christian college culture was just an extension of high school, but at least the goal of finding a husband was more realistic.

I evaluated the "partner potential" of every date I went on. Maybe this guy is the one, and then I can be free. Then I can know I am loved.

This emotional and spiritual state led me to date the "world's worst boyfriends" back-to-back. Because God can redeem literally any situation, there were two silver linings to those dating debacles. The first was that after years of being constantly on the prowl, I was DONE dating for the foreseeable future. The second was that the trauma of my poor choices set the stage for me to fall in love with my husband.

He was not who I had envisioned I would marry. Frankly, he wasn't even my "type." He was skinny, shy, and not at all religious. Surely this wasn't the person sent by God. I lived in the South where the Holy Grail of dating was to find a Campus-Crusade-for-Christ frat boy. Looking back, I have to laugh because I know that type of man would have been a horrible choice for me. Instead, I literally met the boy next door. I had paid zero attention to him in the months that we lived next to each other. One January evening, our neighbors invited me to a poker game at his apartment. He seemed nice enough, but he was kind of drunk, and I didn't go home thinking about him. In fact, I thought he would be a good match for my mathematically-smart roommate. They could nerd out on numbers while I pondered the sociological behavior of college students.

One day, there was a knock on my door, and it was him. He was standing there, and I waited for him to ask for whatever it was that brought him over. It turned out he just wanted to talk … to me. I was confused because he wasn't flirty and put out zero vibes that he wanted a date. We just hung out and talked, and I found myself looking forward to seeing him again, but I wasn't planning our dream wedding like I would have in the past.

One day, I noticed him walking across the parking lot and thought, "*He is cute*." And that was that. Slowly, we began a romantic relationship. After the two previous boyfriends, I was like a stone: hard and suspicious. I was upfront with him that I wasn't looking for casual sex, or really any sex. I expected that would repel him, and this relationship would end before it started, but it didn't faze him at all. What 21-year-old college boy is okay with that boundary? Turns out, a boy with his own issues to sort out. I suspected it might have even been a relief for him. I was intrigued that my Christianity didn't put him off. Surprisingly, he agreed to come to my Bible study and meet with the leader who helped him begin his own relationship with Jesus.

At some point, we broke up. We were so different. My needs were so big, and he just didn't have the capacity to recognize them and "fill my cup." What I wanted, he couldn't give me, and we fought a lot. In the past, no matter how bad a break-up had been, I could always envision my life moving forward. The end of our relationship was different. This time, my future was blank. A gray wall of nothingness in front of me. Now what do I do? I can't see a future without him, but I also think he's a jerk. We stayed broken up for months.

Eventually, we resumed our relationship and had a great summer that year. It was the beginning of our senior year, and time to look past graduation at real life. I was desperate (that's never good) to get engaged and know that my future was secure. Whenever I pressed him on the issue of marriage, he bobbed and weaved like a professional boxer. As graduation neared, I needed to make a decision about where I would attend grad school.

WHAT IS THE PLAN? I can't just float around in the Not-Knowing!!

Do I need to refer back to "The Idol of Marriage" to convey how this situation was about to go off the rails?

He said that if I moved to where he was beginning his job, we would get engaged. So, I followed him, believing that my life would finally start, and my problems would end. I enrolled at an expensive grad school, and he got an apartment and started working. Then, he bought a car and re-established relationships with his old friends. Where was my engagement ring? Apparently, he was driving it.

The bitterness of rejection overtook me. I became snarky, snide, and angry. To add to the negativity, my life was a mess. My parents, my siblings, my schoolwork—I was miserable and lonely. My car sucked, and my internship rejected me for a job and offered it to a fellow student. Also, one of my professors took an immediate dislike to me, making success at school very difficult. Rounding out that terrible year, I graduated without a job, was driving a ten-year-old car with no air conditioning, and I was so poor. To summarize, I was unemployed, not engaged, living with my parents, and cleaning houses for enough cash to put gas in my barely-working car.

I have always blamed the "Year of Misery" on him dragging his feet and taking his time to ask me to marry him. In retrospect, I can understand that he was just settling into adulthood, figuring out finances, and scared of entering into a marriage that could fail. I was waiting for him for my life to start. Of course, these revelations helped me mitigate my deep-seated bitterness … kind of.

We eventually got engaged not long after my graduation and were married five months later. I got what I had been waiting for! Shockingly, this milestone did not solve all of my problems. In fact, getting married seemed to make them worse. We really struggled those first two years, and I began to think I had made a huge mistake. I had put all of my existential eggs into this marriage basket, and my life began unraveling immediately. There was no blissful "honeymoon period." This is what happens when two broken people get together: their problems grow exponentially. Two halves do not equal a whole in marriage.

That's when we had to get to work. Neither one of us wanted a divorce. Now what?

We. Were. Stuck.

Stuck is exactly where you find God patiently waiting for you. I think God is relieved when we become stuck like dinosaurs in the tar pits. It is only then that He can get to work on healing, mending, and redeeming.

Why does complete redemption and total healing take so long? After thirty-one years, I find that I still carry the remnants of bitterness and rejection from those early years.

But.

God loves "buts."

But He can redeem anything—including two immature idiots who got married at twenty-three and twenty-five. We committed ourselves to God and each other without a clue how to keep those promises. God used those times when we had to cry, claw, and struggle as the glue that would hold us together while raising a family. Raising kids is hard, and if we could make it through those early years, we could make it through anything. It has not been easy. Somehow, I have to find a way to unclench my fist and drop those last triggering toxic seeds of bitterness. I needed to look back with an appreciation for all that God had taught and forgiven us. The scars of those early years had only partially healed. I gripped those hurts tightly and used them as weapons against him, and ultimately myself, any time I felt "less than." I had never fully forgiven him.

Analyzing the evolution of our relationship, I can see how one early hurt led to another and another, creating the perfect storm of neediness, loneliness, emptiness, sinfulness, and shame. I tried one hundred ways to heal those wounds and fix the problem. I truly believed that getting married would be the balm that would cover the whole wound, but I didn't need a balm. I needed spiritual surgery.

My only recourse was to turn to God, which is what I thought I had been doing. God knows when our hearts are incomplete, and He waits until we are ready to submit to His will. I do think that if I hadn't gotten married as early as I did, I would have forever been focused on the Idol of Marriage. God gave me what I pleaded for so that He could show me what I actually needed was Him.

Credit: Abigail Keenan (Unsplash)

Musing Twelve
SHAME

Why do so many Christians walk in shame?

Don't we believe in and worship a God who forgives and redeems us?

Who do we allow to be the gatekeepers of God's grace and mercy?

My therapist gave me an assignment to write about shame, as if the six pages I already wrote for her weren't enough. As we debated the semantics of guilt versus shame, she explained that guilt is attached to a singular incident or action, whereas shame is attached to the entirety of a person.

"I did a bad thing" vs "I am a bad person."

Shame shapes how we see ourselves, and then we act accordingly, eyes down, head hung low, praying to go unnoticed as we creep quietly through life. Avoidance seems to be the primary way we cope with our shame. We physically hide from the schoolyard bullies who might mock our hand-me-down clothes or the DIY haircut our moms gave us because money was tight. Material poverty can be reversed quickly. A higher paying job or monetary bonus allows us to replace our threadbare clothes or hunk of crap car. The shame of our physical presentation can be erased.

But what about spiritual shame? We think those wounds are invisible. Adam and Eve thought they were nailing it as the creators of the first game of hide-and-seek. While we may be able to elude the mean girls in the hallway, there is no hiding from God.

And yet.

We try to spiritually hide from God, ourselves, and the people who piled the shame on us in the first place. Shame is always defined and delivered by another person for the purpose of control. If I can impart shame on a person, I am elevated above them, able to manipulate beliefs and behaviors. Wielding shame like a weapon is the primary tool used by so many religious zealots and cult leaders. The prison of shame is patrolled by a warden not interested in your release.

A lot of Christians think shame is the righteous punishment leveled upon us by an angry, legalistic God. We accept the lies of leaders who preach that the masses are unclean and must prostrate themselves before God DAILY to receive a single serving of "forgiveness-manna" that expires when the sun sets. The next morning, we are required to beg God for a new dose because, like drug addicts, we fear a future without the constant foraging for a forgiveness-fix for our shame.

So many of us have fallen victim to the belief that we are eternal sinners and occasional saints. Did Jesus die on the cross for us to continually self-flagellate and flog ourselves? We demean and deny the sacrifice that has already been made when we put ourselves on the cross in His place, thinking that is true penance. If Jesus died for our sins before we even committed them, why do we hold onto our shame as if it is our entrance ticket into heaven?

In Greek mythology, Sisyphus was punished in the afterlife by having to push a huge boulder up a steep hill, only to have it roll back down. He was in a never-ending hell of useless effort and forever frustration. Carrying around the carcass of shame is a Sisyphean task of no reward.

And yet.

We don't live in a Greek tragedy. We can be free. Our freedom isn't earned by lugging around our secret shame in Pandora's box to show our contrition and regret.

Our human nature is to keep our shame locked up tight in the basement of our souls. We crack the door open just enough to feed it but not wide enough to let it escape and be healed. We operate under the belief that shame exposed is exponentially worse than shame contained.

What if the reverse were true? Brené Brown, a noted expert on the study of shame, wisely asserts, "If we can share our story with someone who responds with empathy and understanding, shame can't survive."

What if the "Someone" Brené Brown refers to is Jesus? The Lord who listens with overflowing empathy and understanding and has the ability to heal our shame once and for all, not just for today, but for an eternity.

Psalm 103:12 is an assurance that our mistakes, once forgiven, are not just set aside but utterly removed from our being: *"As far as the east is from the west, so far does He remove our transgressions from us."*

We seem to be resistant to accept how fervently God pursues us. He is desperate for our acknowledgment, acceptance, and admiration of His Holiness. We assume He is repulsed by our shame and sins. I don't think He even concerns Himself with those parts of ourselves until we willingly turn them over to Him. We have to confess it knowing He isn't disappointed or disgusted by us. He separates our whole being from the unsavory parts of ourselves.

> *For the word of God is living and active. Sharper than any two-edged sword, piercing to the division of* **soul and of spirit**, *of joints and of marrow; and discerning thoughts and intentions of the heart. And no creature is hidden from his sight, but all are naked and exposed to the eyes of him to whom we must give account.*
>
> *(Hebrews 4:12—13 NIV)*

He wants us to be healed, healthy, and whole. Our spiritual trash keeps going into the recycle bin instead of a garbage bag to be nailed to the Cross and washed away by the blood of Christ. And I mean AWAY. Gone. No longer there on display. We can be free from shame and filled with the love of God.

> *For we do not have a high priest who is unable to **empathize with our weaknesses**, but we have one who has been tempted in every way, just as we are—yet he did not sin. Let us then approach God's throne of grace with confidence, so that we may receive mercy and find grace to help us in our time of need.*
>
> *(Hebrews 4:15—16 NIV)*

So, why do we resist so mightily?

We cling to our "garbage bag of shame" as if it were the ballast that steadies us. Ballast is a heavy material (often gravel or sand) used to stabilize a ship. However, an airship or hot air balloon must jettison its ballast to reach higher altitudes. We have to readjust our flight calculations without the weight. Would we feel empty-handed without it? Who would we actually be if we let it go and rose to greater heights?

Credit: Yuichi Kageyama (Unsplash)

Musing Thirteen
GOD LOVES BUTS

When I was in college, I had one of "those years." It was not a year of death-by-a-thousand-papercuts, but it was a time of significant grief and loss. I was at the point of telling God I could not take one more thing. My stepfather shared Psalm 13 with me, and it has become one of my favorite chapters in the Bible. The reason I love it, and the Psalms, is because of the *BUTS* and *YETS*.

The Psalms, in particular, contain the raw emotions of the authors. They honestly poured out their fears, anxieties, and torment. We can all relate to feeling left behind, alone, unsafe, and persecuted. The good news for us is that these painful passages make a U-turn at the corner of *BUT* and *YET*.

The word "But" indicates a direct contradiction to the previous statement and is used 150 times in the Psalms alone. David laments in Psalm 13:1, *"How long, O Lord, will you forget me forever?"* For four more verses, David pours out his grief until verse 5. *"BUT I have trusted in your steadfast love;*

my heart shall rejoice in your salvation." David's circumstances didn't change between verses 1 and 5, but his attitude did.

I love the Psalms because the writers are not trying to sugarcoat or dilute their despair. We can't hide from the God who says He knows how many hairs we have on our heads (Luke 12:7). God wants authenticity from us because only then can we share intimacy with Him.

The path out of misery lies in the *BUT.* In Psalm 18:1-18, David paints a vivid picture of how distressed he is until he drops a beautiful *BUT.*

> *"They confronted me in the day of my calamity, BUT the Lord was my support. He brought me out into a broad place. He rescued me because He delighted in me" (vs. 18).*

When I am back in the spiritual wilderness trying to find my way out, I remember the *BUT.*

I am scared, *BUT* God is with me.

I am sad, *BUT* God knows my grief.

Life stinks right now, *BUT* God has promised me better days.

"Yet" indicates a contrast that is a surprise or is counterintuitive to the expected outcome. "Yet" is in the Bible around 400 times.

Psalm 22:1: *"My God, My God, why have you forsaken me?"*

We see this exact expression used by Jesus on the cross. How can we go from feeling forsaken to proclaiming God's goodness? The answer lies with YET. In the same Psalm, David reminds himself and us of this truth:

"*YET you are holy" (vs 3)*.

Both things can be true. We can feel that God is absent from our struggles and know He is holy.

I feel alone, *YET* God is always present.

I feel my faith faltering, *YET* God says to hang on.

I don't understand why this terrible thing is happening, *YET* God says to trust in His Will.

When I am questioning the character of God, I focus on the *YET*. God's character is not dependent on my circumstances, but how I deal with them is dependent on my trust and faith that, *YET,* God is holy.

There is a silly saying, "*If ifs and buts were candy and nuts, what a wonderful world it would be.* "

Instead, we should think about how the *YETs* and *BUTs* make God's kingdom a wonderful place to be.

Credit: Brandon Hoogenboom (Unsplash)

Musing Fourteen
STUCK

Yesterday, I rage-scribbled about how stuck I feel in this season in my life. Stuck in my ways, my weight, my weakness, the weariness, and the wilderness. I feel like my heart intentions are pure in asking (begging) God to move me through this season of stagnation.

The long winter season.

The dry desert season.

No fruit harvested.

No relief from physical pain, insomnia, and a bad attitude.

What is happening under the cold soil of my soul? Anything? Nothing?

Moses was a lonely sheep herder trying to avoid the people who rejected and threatened him, and he was hiding from the sins he had committed. His goal was to live quietly … avoiding detection and drama. Had he lost hope, or was he content with an uneventful life guarding livestock? It didn't matter because that season of his life was never meant to be permanent. Eventually, he was called to an extraordinary task: daily fellowship with God and the chance to lead his people through their wilderness. After all, he had just spent forty years in his own wilderness. You would think he would jump at the chance for excitement and serving God. However, when the Glory of God was upon Moses, he resisted by outlining his reservations:

What do I say?

They won't believe me.

I'm not a good speaker.

Send someone else.

Getting "unstuck" was not what Moses was praying for. At this point in my life, I am asking to get unstuck. Am I missing something? An unconfessed sin that keeps a veil between me and the crystal-clear clarity of God's presence? Am I supposed to remain in the wilderness, wandering and wondering what to do next? For how long?

To be saved from drowning, you must fight the instinct to flail in an effort to save yourself. You must submit to the savior. Be still and be saved. But what if I drown while I sink further below—into the depths of my depression, despair, and disinterest? I gave up the "doing" part years ago. I can't seem to work my way out of the Stuck. I've been dormant like my gardenia bush after a hard winter freeze. Scraggly and producing a scant few leaves but no fragrant flowers. No growth. Just trying to survive with little energy for new leaves or pretty blooms. Do I pull the shrubs or give them another season?

In Ecclesiastes, the seasons of life are detailed. There is a "time to search and a time to give up." Why does my saving grace and salvation come like a last-second lifeline in a thriller?

Will my hope arrive like Indiana Jones rolling under the closing, crushing door by a millisecond? Or will it come early with a large serving of mercy on the side?

I can only cling to the belief that relief and hope are at the end of this season. I have to blindly dive through the crack at the bottom of the cave, not being able to see where it leads.

As I marinated in my STUCK narrative all day yesterday, I became frustrated, bitter, and of course, full of self-pity. This morning, I opened my new devotional to read these words:

> *You will bear fruit in the next season.*
> *You feel stagnant, stale, and stuck.*
> *You wonder if something is wrong—if you've done something wrong.*
> *A deep work has been happening beneath the soil of your life.*
> *A hidden transformation is occurring under the surface.*
> *Increase and enlargement are coming.*
> *You will begin to experience the "more" you have so longed to see.*
> —Craig Cooney, *The Threshold*

Maybe I'm not stuck with my feet in concrete. What if I am inching forward down a long hallway, or sitting in the waiting room listening for my name to be called? What feels like stagnancy is really a preparation for a season of reaping a harvest. For now, I am anxiously waiting to hear His voice guiding me into a season of adventure and abundance.

Credit: Declan Lopez (Unsplash)

Musing Fifteen
SOFT TIRES ON A GRAVEL ROAD

My dad had a distinctive voice, like the smooth sound of soft tires on a gravel road. When he died suddenly on a hot July afternoon, all I could really think to myself was that I would never hear that voice again. The next thought I had was, *Welp, I'd better make an appointment with my therapist!*

I hadn't seen her in a year. It had been a decent year, busy but emotionally peaceful. Well, as emotionally peaceful as a woman standing on the edge of Menopause Mountain and sending her firstborn to college can be. Halfway through our session, she chuckled and said, "You're going to HATE your homework."

Great.

My purpose in seeing her was to hash out the lifelong negativity that surrounded my relationship with my dad. Her assignment was for me to find the blessings in our relationship. I said, "You're right. I already hate it."

To put my relationship with him into perspective, I will start with the day he died. I was having a dinner party and had a house full of guests. As soon as my plate hit the table, I heard my phone ring and saw that it was my brother. He doesn't typically call to chit-chat, so I knew something was up. I walked into the hallway and he said, "We lost Dad today."

I lowered my voice as we discussed basic "housekeeping" details of who to call next. My dad had been married four times. Creating a "phone tree" between the two of us was going to be a Herculean task that I was not physically, nor emotionally, able to do in that moment. I hung up, took a deep breath, shoulders back, chest out — and calmly took my seat back at the dinner table as if nothing had happened. Because in almost no way did his passing impact my immediate life, although I knew I'd have to "process it" emotionally at some point. Six weeks later, I was completing my homework by writing a letter to my dad thanking him. Ouch.

My dad spent the first twelve years of his life stained with Tennessee red clay, and the remaining sixty years trying to wash it off. He was the odd man out in his family. Simple, uneducated hill people with not many social graces were his roots. My dad was intellectual, sensitive, and not at all athletic. He had the vision and wisdom to know that the only way out of his social and financial standing and off the Ford assembly line was to go to college, a goal his father frowned upon and did not support.

At Eastern Michigan University, he met my mother, who was also sensitive, bookish, and not athletic. They got married, had a baby, and took turns working to pay each other's tuition. My mother was one year ahead of him in college. He deferred his classes and worked on the Ford assembly line (with his father) for a year so she could graduate. In turn, she went to work, and he graduated the following year.

Growing up, one of the things I knew was expected of me was that I was to get good grades and go to college. The other thing I began to "know" was that my dad did not like kids. His or anyone else's. Rejection by a parent cuts a chasm that is so deep and so wide that only the love of God can begin to fill the void.

We didn't start off that badly, but over the years, the rift grew, and with it my bitterness and his inability to be a dad. He was a "father"; dutifully picking us up every other weekend per their custody agreement, but he didn't spend time with us. We occupied ourselves with our step-siblings and the TV. We could watch anything we wanted and for as many hours/days as we wanted, as long as we weren't bugging him. We just never "got" each other. When he picked us up for the weekend, as we pulled into the garage, I would turn to him and ask, "When are you taking me home?"

I didn't mean this as an insult; I was a terribly anxious child who missed my mom. I simply wanted to know when I was going home again. To his fragile ego and insecure self, this question felt like rejection. We continued this dance until I was almost thirteen.

Then, with almost no warning, he left the East Coast and moved to California. After that, I saw him once, maybe twice a year. He was often back in town for business, but I began to discover that more often than not, he wouldn't tell me when he was near. I guess once a year was good enough for him. We continued this dance until the day he died.

At almost every fork in the road, he made deliberate choices to avoid seeing my brother and me. This went on for decades. At some point, when you've had enough rejection, you just close up that piece of your heart. My brother was more freely giving of himself and was able to be in the moment with my dad. Not me. I had to wall off that piece of my heart and soul that longed to be a Daddy's Girl. Over the years, he would often say I was the "apple of his eye" and "Daddy's Girl," words that fell so hollow in my ears that I could no longer listen to them. Actions spoke louder than words.

My neighbor once told me that "God wastes nothing." It is true. What I learned was that words with no action are really just manipulation. Words with actions to support them are reaffirming and reinforcing. Eventually, I became a girl with high standards after I worked out all the damage of having "Daddy Issues." Once I had my own children, I became even less understanding of his rejection. My kids really are the apple of my eye. I love them so deeply and dearly that I cannot fathom a world in which I would drive past their homes and not stop to see them.

Moving forward, how do I process this? I guess the truth is, I'll never fully understand why he just could not be available. The question that will ring in my ears forever is, "Why didn't he love me?" Over time, I began to fully understand that he never received the love and nurturing from his own abusive and neglectful parents. His childhood trauma did offer me an explanation as to why he was unable to enjoy being a father, but it did not excuse his behavior.

I did do the homework my therapist gave me. It wasn't as hard as I thought. In the end, I hope to remember my dad as the person who taught me it's okay to leave the butter on the counter, there's no such thing as overdoing Christmas, and that education and discipline are the cornerstones for success in almost every aspect of life. Lastly, most importantly, I learned to raise my kids feeling loved, wanted, and enjoyed.

Credit: Priscila Reis

Musing Sixteen
HIM

I was so young that I don't remember the first time I met "HIM." My parents divorced when I was only three years old, so I was accustomed to having my mother mostly to myself. I do remember the exact moment they came into my room to announce their intention to marry. My reaction was swift and angry.

"HE" was going to ruin everything. My mother and I had a good thing going. Why did she need or want to get married, especially to someone my six-year-old self deemed unacceptable?

It was a wreck from day one. I was a stubborn and surly child, longing for love and attention from my own emotionally-distant father. My stepfather was heartbroken and desperate to see his own sons regularly, which was not happening. We both were longing for our relationships to be healed and restored, but instead, we were stuck with each other.

Some relationships flow like a river, and I am blessed to have a few—so effortless, mutually beneficial, and deeply satisfying. Then there are the relationships like jagged rocks with peaks and valleys and often sharp edges. However, what can happen is that the proverbial "water under the bridge" can slowly smooth over those jagged rocks, and you end up with something more like the Grand Canyon; eternally deep, wild, and ultimately beautiful.

Studies have shown that it can take an average of ten years for a blended (i.e. broken) family to mend and meld, and that is about how long it took before I began to accept that this irritating interloper had become an ally. As I got older, we found common ground on the tiniest things like *The Far Side* comic strip or humor writer Dave Barry's weekly newspaper column. We would howl with laughter while my humor-challenged mother looked on in bewilderment. The tide turned even more when I returned home after college. Our schedules left us usually eating lunch together while we quietly listened to talk radio. It became something of a ritual, and we were annoyed on the days my mother intruded on this time.

As the years went on, I began to realize that my own father would be forever limited in his ability to love and support me in the way a daughter is desperate for. My heart of stone towards "HIM" began to soften, and I began to silently accept that he had become my "dad." HE rescued me from my broken-down car in the dark, we found common interests, discussed politics, occasionally ganged up on my eccentric mother, and I fed him the baked goods he craved that we rarely had in the house.

When I was pregnant with my first child, HE was the one who drove me and a car full of baby shower gifts ten hours back home. He stayed a while; we went to a play and out to eat before he flew home. It was just "normal," like how normal families are. It was HIM I was talking to on the phone when my water broke in a hospital ten hours away, and I said, "Uh … you better get in the car NOW."

Without any announcement, formal decree, or fanfare, our decades-long battle became a quiet understanding, and eventually it became just "family"— comfortable, easy, and loving.

We were not a close family. Fractured is putting it politely. My parents' philosophy was to "divide and conquer," and as a result, my own brother and I were kept separate from our four stepbrothers. I suspect my stepfather couldn't handle dealing with the emotions of parenting six wildly different kids at the same time. Decades have passed where the only communication between most of us was a Christmas card.

But then "Dad" got sick six weeks ago. The six of us made a pact to fully communicate all the details to each other. A group text thread, email chain, and conference calls began. A cord of six strings is hard to break. We each had different jobs and roles to manage my mother and their father. My brothers have "kid gloves"; they are kind, loving, and do things respectfully. As the only girl and probably the feistiest of all of us, I employ "boxing gloves." I step in and start kicking butt and taking names when the people surrounding my parents need a hard shove in the right direction. Sometimes, I had to battle my parents themselves to be reasonable and logical.

So here I am, the morning after he died, sitting at my kitchen table, choking back tears as I am bombarded by the memories of someone who was a giant part of my heart. He loved ice cream, well-done steaks, chocolate, *A Christmas Story*, playing tennis, and the Washington Redskins. He hated squirrels and throwing away any morsel of food. This grief hit so differently than when my own father passed away four years earlier. This time, I had lost the man who had actually become my "dad."

Fortunately, In HIS later years, he was finally able to have a deep closeness with his own sons as the wounds of divorce and their childhood hurts healed. Now HE is gone. The sadness and grief each of us felt are hard to put into words. I read an analogy that explains that when we look at our lives, it looks like the backside of a needlepoint tapestry, a mess of tangled threads and knots seemingly without order. What God sees is the flip side. All of that mess and chaos becomes something beautiful when seen through God's eyes. My family weathered deep hurts from the dysfunction we endured, but I believe that with time and God's grace, those jagged edges have become smooth, and the water flows freely and easily over them.

Credit: The Chaffins (Unsplash)

Musing Seventeen
FORGIVENESS: THE OTHER "F" WORD

For over fifty years, I struggled to let go of the bitterness and what-ifs that I kept in the vault of my spirit, that part of myself I could not release to God. I often wondered, *"What could I have been if my family had been healthier and functional?"* I battled jealousy when I saw the freedom my children had to flourish into who they chose to be. *How much potential did I have that got lost in the sea of negativity I struggled to climb out of?* I knew that forgiveness was crucial to being able to move forward, but I hit a brick wall every time I tried to let go of this fantasy that if things had been different, I would have been so much "more" than I was. I recognize how egotistical that fantasy sounds, but it was easier to blame my parents than accept who I was.

Forgiveness has always been a weakness of mine. A garden of "anger" weeds had grown in my heart. As I pondered how I would prune myself of these poisonous plants, I realized that I was the one keeping myself from my full potential. I could no longer blame my parents. When I set out to journal my feelings, it also became apparent that I was angry at God. He was the one who put me in this situation to begin with. If God doesn't make mistakes, how could I reconcile all that had transpired as being part of His Plan? Turns out that God's character isn't dependent on my circumstances. The following "conversation" is what flowed from my pencil.

Carmen: My therapist says I have to forgive my parents.

God: Yes, you do.

C: But I don't want to.

G: You don't have to want to. Jesus didn't want to go to the cross, but He did it out of obedience to My Plan and His love for Me. He trusted Me, even on the cross. You can trust me with your pain as well.

C: I felt so alone with no power or advocate.

G: As a parent, you have witnessed your own children struggling with an issue you could have "fixed," but you didn't, knowing the struggle and fight was essential for their growth. The pain was the price of the lesson. They weren't alone, either. You were there, watching and choosing not to intervene. As a child, you weren't alone. It hurt Me to see you hurting. I had to forge you in the fire. Some people are put together delicately … they are beautiful but fragile, like a bird. I wanted you to be strong and stubborn … like a donkey 😊 . You had to be broken and welded back together because I knew the load you would have to bear.

C: But that pain and those experiences made me a worse person who made bad choices and had poor boundaries. A bit of a loser and a bigger sinner. What more could I have been if I hadn't been so damaged?

G: This is how I wanted you. You see this as lame. I brought you here specifically for this time. As for bad decisions, you can only blame your parents so much. Ultimately, you made the choice to sin. In your heart, you knew you were doing wrong. Maybe their behavior laid the foundation, but you were the bricklayer. When you prayed, I forgave you for those heinous acts and hateful thoughts. I brought you to a place of prosperity and blessings. Did you deserve it? No. But you are my child, and I want great things for you, just like you want your kids to be happy, independent, and virtuous. That destination can only be reached through dangerous and difficult trials. My love is bigger than your mistakes and theirs. No mistake on anyone's part will cause Me to withdraw My Love. It was your choice to separate from Me.

C: Because I didn't see or trust you when I was a child. I still struggle to trust You now.

G: Should your kids trust you? You've let them flounder and fail on purpose. Your love is imperfect. Mine is perfect.

C: Your way seems cruel at times.

G: You can have your opinions, but it doesn't change anything. Ask Job. You don't have to understand or like it. You do have to submit to it.

C: Ha. Your choice of parents and my childhood experiences specifically made me fight submission.

G: I don't want you to submit to people or the world. You needed that hard shell so you wouldn't be swept up with blind followers or accept bad theology. It's time to learn the difference between submitting to Me versus the world. You wanted your children to heed your advice, not their friends', right? Every parent wants their kids to be able to hold strong in the face of adversity—to be able to think and act for themselves, even if it goes against the cultural grain.

C: If I submit and try to forgive them and let my anger go, does that mean they got away with their bad judgment and behavior?

G: First, you are not qualified to judge people. Second, you have to trust that in your obedience and submission, I can change anything. Their sins can't be reversed until you let them go. I'm glad I raised you to be a fighter, but now you are only fighting yourself, like an autoimmune disease. You've become self-destructive.

C: This is going to be hard. I'll have to work on it for a while. The enemy will keep offering me the bitterness on a platter. It has been my sustenance for my whole life. What if I disappear when I stop eating it?

G: I am The Way, The Truth, and The Light. Has this meal of malcontent kept you nourished and healing? Doritos and Coke will give you enough calories to stay alive … but yuck.

C: True. Though Doritos and Coke taste good initially, eventually, they eat you alive on the inside. All my life, I have known I was an "accident," not planned by my parents. However, I was wanted by the Creator. In the end, my father was glad I was born, even though he was not at all equipped to be a father. There were generations of monsters raising monsters.

G: They weren't monsters. They were broken and didn't know where to turn. I created you to break that cycle, knowing it wouldn't be easy for you. Jesus was a sacrifice for mankind. You were a sacrifice for your future descendants. You passed the test, and now your kids won't know the generational pain that you and your brother do. For that, you should be grateful. You always say you see yourself like Gandalf from *The Lord of the Rings*, standing on the bridge telling the demon, "You shall not pass." You would happily take on that battle for your own children. You would sacrifice your life for theirs, right?

C: Of course.

G: Okay, you already did. You HAD to go through those years and all that pain to spare them. If you see it as a sacrifice for your kids, it takes the sting and resentment away from your parents.

C: You know, I always struggle with your sense of timing.

G: That's okay. You don't have to like it. You just have to trust it.

C: If I can see those past times as a sacrifice I had to make for the kids that I love now, that helps. But I was so young. Jesus had grown and understood the mission He had agreed to complete.

G: It had to happen while you were still becoming a person. Clay is easiest to shape when it's soft, not dry and hard. Trying to mold an adult requires a lot more pain. Frankly, you should be grateful. This is what the sacrifice of praise is, my Love.

C: When you frame it like that, I am glad you molded me when you did. So, why do I feel dry and hard now?

G: You're questioning my timing again.

C: Okay, I forgive them because it meant freedom for my kids and wisdom for me. Didn't Solomon say that wisdom was more precious than gold?

G: Now you're starting to get it.

Credit: Tori Tan (Unsplash)

Musing Eighteen
DON'T LOOK BACK ...
ANYMORE

I was reading a book about spiritual growth, and I came to a section titled, *"I Don't Do Introspection."* What? I have spent the bulk of my adult life looking inside and backwards, pondering and analyzing questions like:

Was that my fault?
Did I cause trouble?
Does anyone even like me?
Why was I so rude, bitter, or angry with that person?

As I got older, the focus of my introspection also turned to my parents.

Why did they do that?
How can I be different?
I don't want to be like_____.
I don't want to do _____.

My husband is obsessed with golf; it is his favorite topic. Once, after a visit with his father, he came home to tell me why he was frustrated after playing golf with him.

He said, "Right before I was going to hit my ball, my dad said, 'Don't hit the ball into the water.'" Guess where the ball landed? Right in the drink.

Why? The directive had been clear. Don't hit the ball into the water. What's the issue? Think about it; the last words he heard were "hit the ball into the water." The *don't* got diluted. When we spend a lot of time focusing on what we don't want to do or be, we end up struggling with those exact issues. Oftentimes, people will enter adulthood thinking, *"I don't want to be like (insert influential adult)."* While I don't think this line of contemplation is inherently bad or unproductive, a tremendous amount of energy is spent on how NOT to be: lazy, aggressive, bad with money, adulterous, abusive, etc. The list goes on forever. At some point, enough self-reflection has occurred, and it's time to focus on what I **_can_** be.

Even the Old Testament, written thousands of years ago, speaks to the dangers of living in the past.

In Ecclesiastes 3, there is a list of the seasons of life, acknowledging there is a time for almost everything, including "a time to tear and a time to sew" (vs 7). Think about your past enough to formulate a future, and then let it go.

In Genesis, Lot's wife was turned into a pillar of salt for disobeying the Lord's command not to turn back as she was fleeing the destruction of Sodom. Whether you read that anecdote as a parable or a literal account, the message is the same. As God was delivering her from certain death, and she took a final glance behind her, the Lord said, "Escape for your life. Do not look back or stop … lest you be swept away" (Genesis 19:17).

The temptation for more contemplation can be an unseen rip tide of ruin. People in shallow water have been swept out to sea by the invisible force of the water. Many beaches will fly flags warning swimmers that a rip tide is present. The problem is, the exhortation isn't heeded because we can't see the potential for harm. I bet if we could see a giant shark fin poking ominously out of the water, we would likely stick to shore. Ironically, ten times more people die annually from rip tides than from shark attacks.

Sometimes the unseen snares can be the deadliest. Many families display certain negative "patterns" throughout the generations—discord, addiction, alcoholism. The logical assumption would be to focus your energy on NOT perpetuating those toxic behaviors and becoming a "cycle-breaker"—the one who gets to hit the familial reset button so future generations can grow in health and freedom. The concept that this can best be done by divorcing yourself from the past and constructing a fresh paradigm is new to me.

I have a bachelor's degree in social work with minors in psychology and sociology, and a master's degree in social work with a concentration in child and adolescent behavior. I was made for constant evaluation, analysis, and adjustment. I am naturally fascinated by people, group behavior, family dynamics, and social interactions. Therefore, when I got to the section about not engaging in introspection, I was intrigued. I had believed that the key to making sure history did not repeat itself was keeping my eyes focused solely on the rearview mirror. Of course, if we really drove a car that way, we'd smash into whatever is ahead of us, leading to costly damage and a delay arriving at our destination. When we drive, we do have to take cursory glances at what is behind us, but we can't fix our eyes there.

A quick Pinterest search of quotes about not looking back yielded these results:

- ❖ *Never run back to what broke you. Once you make the decision to move on, don't look back. Your destiny will never be found in the rearview mirror*—Mandy Hale

- ❖ *Dear Past, thanks for the lessons. Dear Future, I'm ready now.*—Unknown

- ❖ *Too much looking backwards is bad for progress*—Henry Ward Beecher

I believe that we have to acknowledge and come to terms with our past, and then there comes a time to close those chapters and write a new future. Healing past hurts can feel like playing Whack-A-Mole; as soon as you deal with one, another pops up. The trick is to practice knocking down that negative issue, accept it as healed, and move on. I've spent decades concerning myself with who I don't want to be, and maybe in the process, I forgot to figure out who God says that I am.

Who does God say that I am? Am I a sinner or a saint? Am I a spiritual orphan or a child of God? In his book *Classic Christianity*, Bob George says, *"If you were to see a butterfly, it would never occur to you to say, 'Hey, everybody! Come look at this good-looking converted worm!' And it was 'converted.' No, now it is a new creature, and you don't think of it in terms of what it was. You see it as it is now—a butterfly.*

In exactly the same way, God sees you as His new creature in Christ. Although you might not always act like a good butterfly—you might land on things you shouldn't, or forget you are a butterfly and crawl around with your old worm buddies—the truth of the matter is, you are never going to be a worm again!"

I appreciate the irony that I just wrote an entire book on how hard it can be to move forward. It is time for me to take my own advice and stop acting like a "converted worm" so I can fly freely like a butterfly.

Who wants to join me?

Therefore, if anyone is in Christ, the new creation has come: The old has gone, the new is here!
2 Corinthians 5:17

Acknowledgments

This book would still be in a folder on my desk if it weren't for the persistent prodding of Dr. Trudy Simmons. She saw beauty where there were ashes and emboldened me to share my writing so that it would glorify God and resonate with hurting people.

Missy Maxwell Worton has been my own personal cheerleader, championing me with confidence and pushing me to be a better writer.

Thank you to my Beta readers: Kelly Fredrickson and Steve New. Your honest feedback means the world to me.

Thank you to the Light Warrior Writers; you all inspire me to improve and grow as a writer.

Thank you, Donna Bess, for editing what was probably a grammatical nightmare and turning my book into something I can be proud of.

Thank you, Tammy Largin, for designing the book cover because I do not have an artistic bone in my body.

Despite the fact that I am perpetually cranky, I have the best friends anyone could want. They are honest, hilarious, real, and they stand by me regardless of my attitude.

My WAB crew, no one provides me with more laughter, tears of joy, deep talks, and companionship. I love you 3000.

My Highcroft Moms, you have been my literal lifeline, the village that raised my kids, kept me "sane" and the shoulders I leaned on. No one is luckier than me to have all of you.

EOD, you tolerate me daily. Being your friend is a privilege, and you are stuck with me.

My brothers (the "brotatoes"), you are kind-hearted, godly men whose best characteristic is that you all laugh easily and heartily. You guys "get it" because you lived it. No one else would understand that a sand-stuffed squirrel is the least of what we experienced.

My sister, Aimee, is my best friend since we were four years old. We all need a truth teller, a BS-caller and someone on our side no matter what. I am the lucky one.

My children, Ginger, Christian and Brittany, there is no version of my life I would want without you in it. Everything I needed to learn about life, God, forgiveness and growth, I learned from you. You are my sunshine.

To my husband, without your love, support and computer skills, this book would be lost somewhere on my laptop. You fulfilled dreams I never dared to dream.

Bibliography

Brown, Brené. *Daring Greatly: How the Courage to be Vulnerable Transforms the Way We Live, Love, Parent, and Lead.* (Gotham Books 2012).

Cooney, Craig. *The Threshold.* (DP Publishing 2024).

George, Bob. *Classic Christianity: Life's Too Short to Miss the Real Thing.* (Harvest House Publishing 2012).

Leman, Kevin. *The Birth Order Book: Why You Are the Way You Are.* (F. H. Revell 2004).

Rosemond, John. *The Well Behaved Child: Discipline That Really Works!* (Thomas Nelson 2009).

Spurgeon, Charles H. *Morning and Evening.* (Ligonier Ministries 2023).

Williams, Margery. *The Velveteen Rabbit.* (Egmont Books 2004).